As families take control of the symptoms of ADHD and bring out the best in their child, they become happier and parenting becomes more fun.

AGES: 10-13 years old

Raising a child with ADHD can be distressing and exhausting for the whole family. This simple, flexible step-by-step programme will help parents to manage their child's behaviour, leading to improved relationships at home and create a more successfull and settled time at school/educational institutions.

This is very basic and teach the children discipline and the emphasis is stimulation of as much body awareness as possible.

Programme schedule for the treatment of ADHD.

This is an easy schedule to follow and usually takes 20 minutes per session.

Week 1:
Do sketches 1-6 , Monday - Friday.

Week 2:
Do sketches 7-12, Monday - Friday.

Week 3:
Do sketches 12-18, Monday - Friday.

Week 4:
Do sketches 19-25, Monday - Friday.

Week 5:
Do sketches 26-30, Monday - Friday.

Week 6:
Do sketches 31-35, Monday - Friday.

Week 7:
Do sketches 36-40, Monday - Friday.

After you have finished the programme, you can repeat the programme as needed, until your child turns 14 years of age.

TEK 1

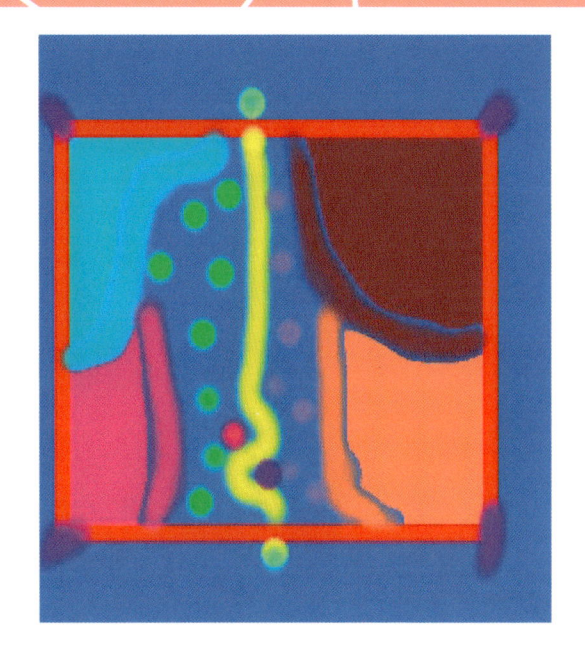

1. Sit comfortable and breathe mindfully for 3 seconds.

2. Close your right eye and look at the light blue object for 13 seconds.

3. Close your left eye and look at the pink object for 13 seconds.

4. Look with both eyes open at the small pink and small purple balls for 20 seconds.

5. Look with both eyes open at the yellow line for 3 seconds.

6. Close your right eye and look at the orange object for 13 seconds.

7. Close your left eye and look at the brown object for 13 seconds.

8. Close your eyes and breathe mindfully for 3 seconds.

TEK 2

1. Sit comfortable and breathe mindfully for 3 seconds.

2. Close your right eye and look at the blue heart for 20 seconds.

3. Close your left eye and look at the blue heart for 20 seconds.

4. Look with both eyes open at the dark blue lining around the blue heart for 21 seconds.

5. Look with both eyes open pink lining around the red heart for 21 seconds.

6. Close your right eye and look at the red heart for 27 seconds.

7. Close your left eye and look at the red heart for 27 seconds.

8. Close your eyes and breathe mindfully for 3 seconds.

TEK 3

1. Sit comfortable and breathe mindfully for 2 seconds.

2. Close your right eye and look at the big blue balloon for 27 seconds.

3. Close your left eye and look at the small blue balloon for 27 seconds.

4. Look with both eyes open at the salmon pink balloon for 7 seconds.

5. Look with both eyes open at the red lines for 7 seconds.

6. Close your right eye and look at the bright pink balloons for 27 seconds.

7. Close your left eye and look at the bright pink balloons for 27 seconds.

8. Close your eyes and breathe mindfully for 3 seconds.

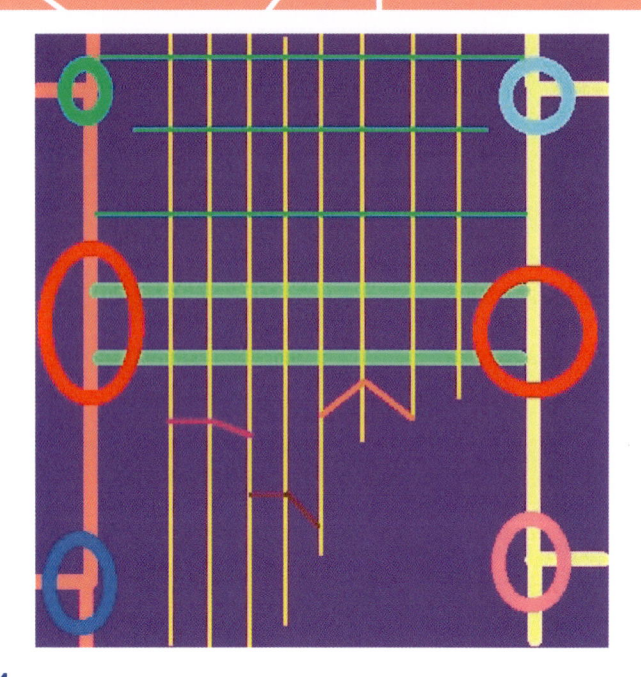

TEK 4

1. Sit comfortable and breathe mindfully for 2 seconds.

2. Close your right eye and look at the light blue circle for 6 seconds.

3. Close your left eye and look at the dark blue circle for 6 seconds.

4. Look with both eyes open at the small green circle for 12 seconds.

5. Look with both eyes open at the two green lines for 12 seconds.

6. Close your right eye and look at the small red circle for 6 seconds.

7. Close your left eye and look at the big red circle for 6 seconds.

8. Close your eyes and breathe mindfully for 2 seconds.

TEK 5

1. Sit comfortable and breathe mindfully for 7 seconds.

2. Close your right eye and look at the light blue ball for 17 seconds.

3. Close your left eye and look at the light blue ball for 17 seconds.

4. Look with both eyes open at the purple ball for 10 seconds.

5. Look with both eyes open at the blue ball for 10 seconds.

6. Close your right eye and look at the yellow ball for 17 seconds.

7. Close your left eye and look at yellow ball for 17 seconds.

8. Close your eyes and breathe mindfully for 7 seconds.

TEK 6

1. Sit comfortable and breathe mindfully for 5 seconds.

2. Close your right eye and look at the small blue window for 5 seconds.

3. Close your left eye and look at the small blue window for 5 seconds.

4. Look with both eyes open at the red object for 5 seconds.

5. Look with both eyes open at the yellow X for 5 seconds.

6. Close your right eye and look at green object for 5 seconds.

7. Close your left eye and look at the green object for 5 seconds.

8. Close your eyes and breathe mindfully for 5 seconds.

TEK 7

1. Sit comfortable and breathe mindfully for 2 seconds.

2. Close your right eye and look at the light blue block for 3 seconds.

3. Close your left eye and look at the light blue block for 13 seconds.

4. Look with both eyes open at the blue block on the right for 4 seconds.

5. Look with both eyes open at the grey block for 3 seconds.

6. Close your right eye and look at the white block for 5 seconds.

7. Close your left eye and look at the white block for 5 seconds.

8. Close your eyes and breathe mindfully for 6 seconds.

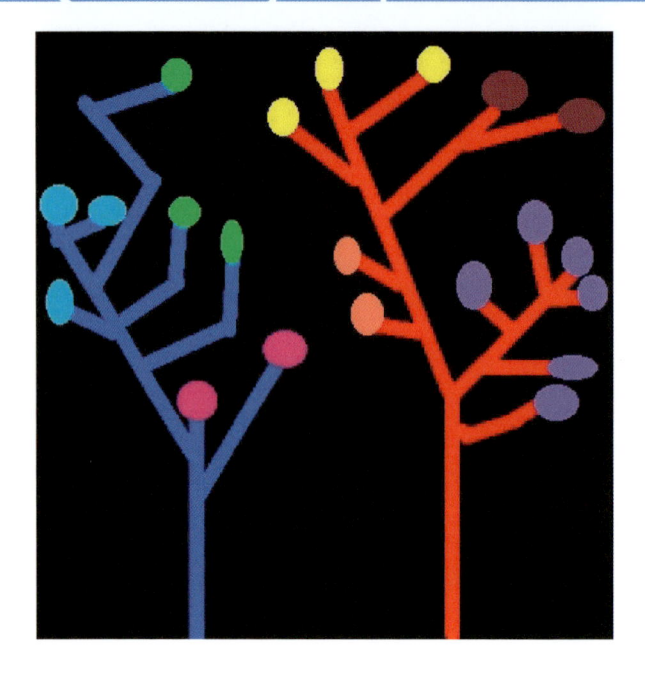

TEK 8

1. Sit comfortable and breathe mindfully for 6 seconds.

2. Close your right eye and look at the pink balls for 16 seconds.

3. Close your left eye and look at the green balls for 13 seconds.

4. Look with both eyes open at the blue tree for 26 seconds.

5. Look with both eyes open at the red tree for 26 seconds.

6. Close your right eye and look at the purple balls for 13 seconds.

7. Close your left eye and look at the yellow balls for 16 seconds.

8. Close your eyes and breathe mindfully for 3 seconds.

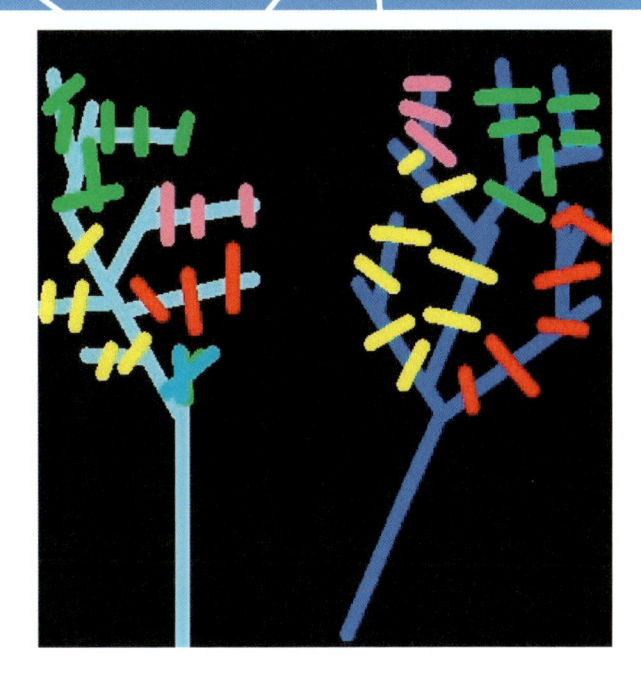

TEK 9

1. Sit comfortable and breathe mindfully for 6 seconds.

2. Close your right eye and look at the yellow lines on the left for 7 seconds.

3. Close your left eye and look at the yellow lines on the right for 7 seconds.

4. Look with both eyes open at the light blue tree for 10 seconds.

5. Look with both eyes open at the blue tree on the right for 10 seconds.

6. Close your right eye and look at the red lines on the left for 8 seconds.

7. Close your left eye and look at the red lines on the right for 8 seconds.

8. Close your eyes and breathe mindfully for 6 seconds.

TEK 10

1. Sit comfortable and breathe mindfully for 7 seconds.

2. Close your right eye and look at the blue object for 9 seconds.

3. Close your left eye and look at the blue object for 9 seconds.

4. Look with both eyes open at the red circle for 8 seconds.

5. Look with both eyes open at the yellow circle for 8 seconds.

6. Close your right eye and look at the black object for 10 seconds.

7. Close your left eye and look at the black object for 10 seconds.

8. Close your eyes and breathe mindfully for 11 seconds.

TEK 11

1. Sit comfortable and breathe mindfully for 12 seconds.

2. Close your right eye and look at the blue object for 13 seconds.

3. Close your left eye and look at the blue object for 13 seconds.

4. Look with both eyes open at the green line for 20 seconds.

5. Look with both eyes open at the green line for 30 seconds.

6. Close your right eye and look at the yellow line for 14 seconds.

7. Close your left eye and look at the yellow line for 14 seconds.

8. Close your eyes and breathe mindfully for 9 seconds.

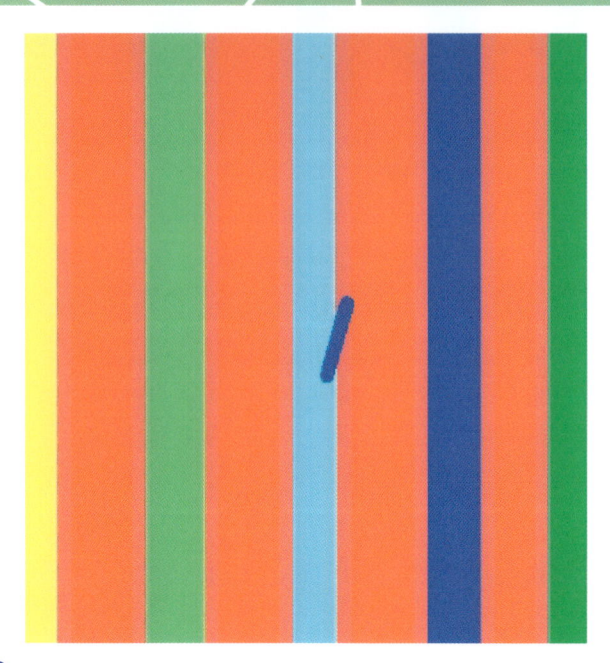

TEK 12

1. Sit comfortable and breathe mindfully for 14 seconds.

2. Close your right eye and look at the light blue line for 15 seconds.

3. Close your left eye and look at the dark blue line for 15 seconds.

4. Look with both eyes open at the light green line for 16 seconds.

5. Look with both eyes open at the small blue line for 16 seconds.

6. Close your right eye and look at the green line for 17 seconds.

7. Close your left eye and look at the yellow line for 13 seconds.

8. Close your eyes and breathe mindfully for 14 seconds.

TEK 13

1. Sit comfortable and breathe mindfully for 18 seconds.

2. Close your right eye and look at the yellow rectangle for 9 seconds.

3. Close your left eye and look at the red square for 9 seconds.

4. Look with both eyes open at the orange glasses for 18 seconds.

5. Look with both eyes open at the red line for 18 seconds.

6. Close your right eye and look at the green e for 20 seconds.

7. Close your left eye and look at the green e for 20 seconds.

8. Close your eyes and breathe mindfully for 10 seconds.

TEK 14

1. Sit comfortable and breathe mindfully for 17 seconds.

2. Close your right eye and look at the boxing glove for 13 seconds.

3. Close your left eye and look at the boxing glove for 13 seconds.

4. Look with both eyes open at the green object with the brown object in the middle for 18 seconds.

5. Look with both eyes open at the pink E for 18 seconds.

6. Close your right eye and look at the apple for 19 seconds.

7. Close your left eye and look at the apple for 19 seconds.

8. Close your eyes and breathe mindfully for 17 seconds.

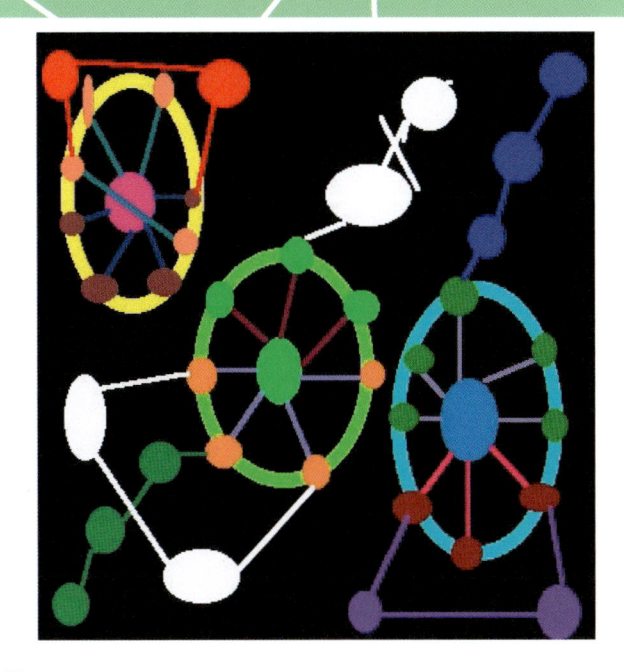

TEK 15

1. Sit comfortable and breathe mindfully for 10 seconds.

2. Close your right eye and look at the light blue wheel for 10 seconds.

3. Close your left eye and look at the green wheel for 10 seconds.

4. Look with both eyes open at the orange balls for 20 seconds.

5. Look with both eyes open at the white balls for 20 seconds.

6. Close your right eye and look at the red balls for 10 seconds.

7. Close your left eye and look at the yellow wheel for 10 seconds.

8. Close your eyes and breathe mindfully for 8 seconds.

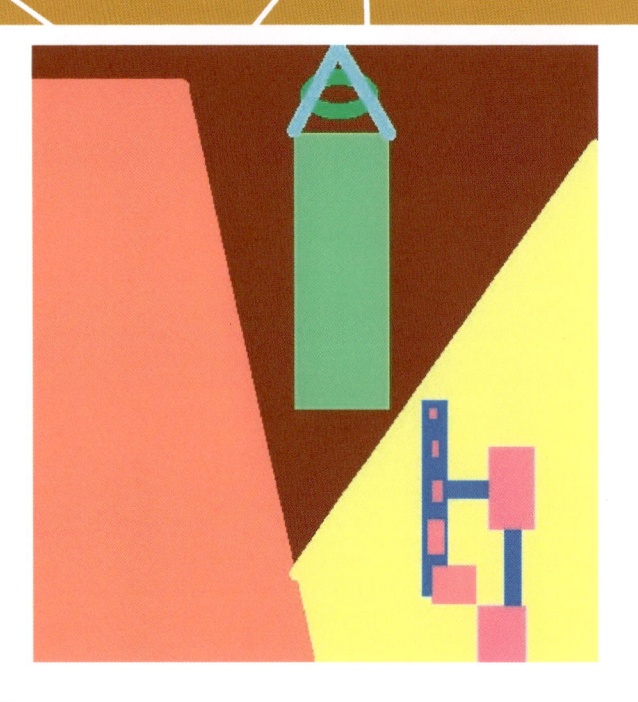

TEK 16

1. Sit comfortable and breathe mindfully for 11 seconds.

2. Close your right eye and look at the green block for 13 seconds.

3. Close your left eye and look at the green block for 13 seconds.

4. Look with both eyes open at the small pink blocks for 12 seconds.

5. Look with both eyes open at the brown object for 12 seconds.

6. Close your right eye and look at the light blue object on the small green circle for 14 seconds.

7. Close your left eye and look at the yellow object for 14 seconds.

8. Close your eyes and breathe mindfully for 9 seconds.

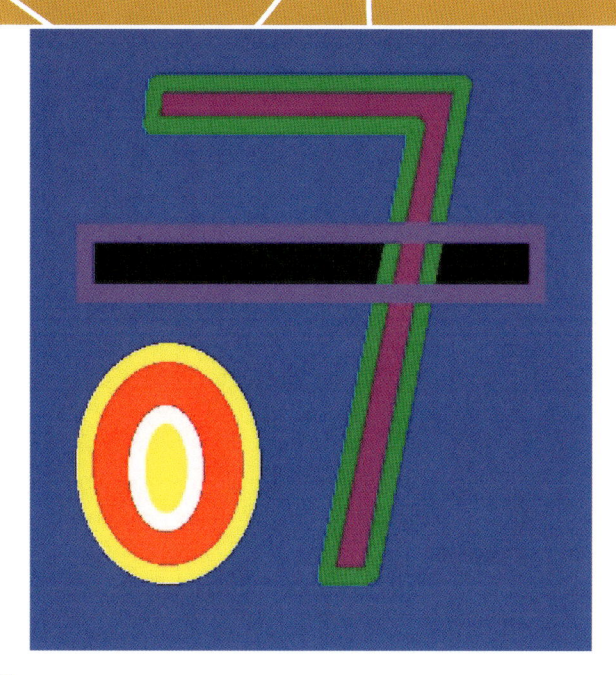

TEK 17

1. Sit comfortable and breathe mindfully for 15 seconds.

2. Close your right eye and look at the purple 7 for 15 seconds.

3. Close your left eye and look at the small white circle for 15 seconds.

4. Look with both eyes open at the big yellow circle for 10 seconds.

5. Look with both eyes open at the red circle for 5 seconds.

6. Close your right eye and look at the green 7 for 15 seconds.

7. Close your left eye and look at the green 7 for 15 seconds.

8. Close your eyes and breathe mindfully for 15 seconds

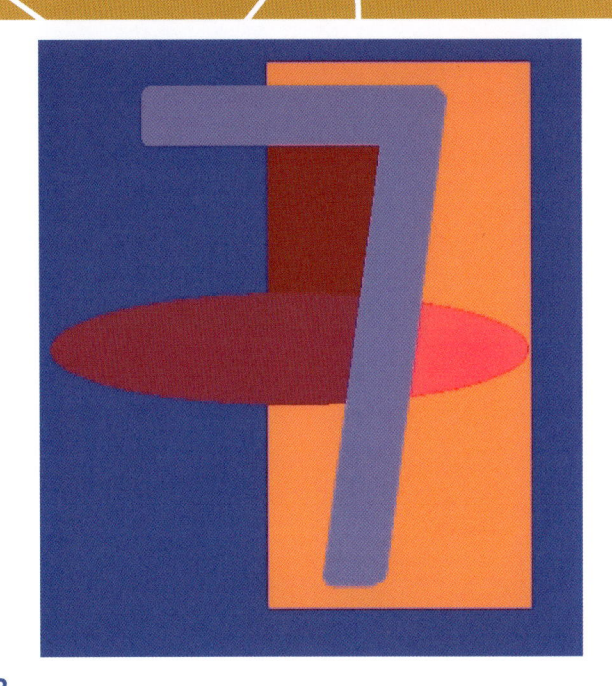

TEK 18

1. Sit comfortable and breathe mindfully for 16 seconds.

2. Close your right eye and look at the orange object for 13 seconds.

3. Close your left eye and look at the orange object for 13 seconds.

4. Look with both eyes open at the pink object for 17 seconds.

5. Look with both eyes open at the brown object for 17 seconds.

6. Close your right eye and look at the purple 7 for 13 seconds.

7. Close your left eye and look at the purple 7 for 13 seconds.

8. Close your eyes and breathe mindfully for 9 seconds.

TEK 19

1. Sit comfortable and breathe mindfully for 18 seconds.

2. Close your right eye and look at the blue object for 8 seconds.

3. Close your left eye and look at the blue object for 8 seconds.

4. Look with both eyes open at the pink star for 6 seconds.

5. Look with both eyes open at the bright pink object for 6 seconds.

6. Close your right eye and look at the red ball for 8 seconds.

7. Close your left eye and look at the red ball for 8 seconds.

8. Close your eyes and breathe mindfully for 18 seconds

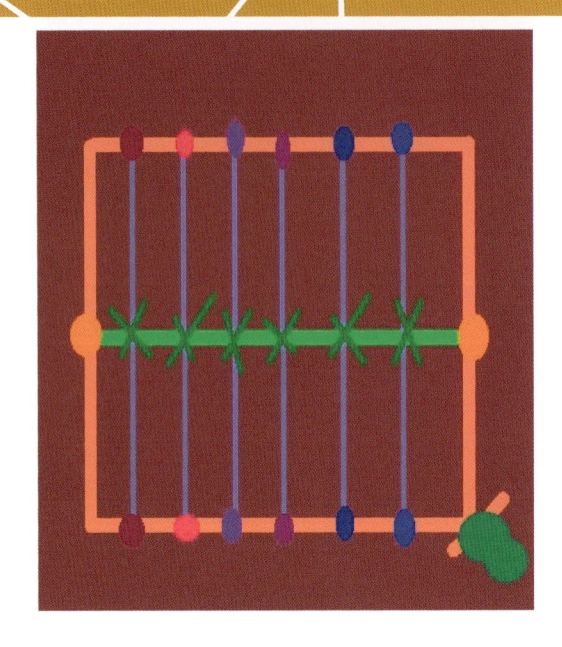

TEK 20

1. Sit comfortable and breathe mindfully for 20 seconds.

2. Close your right eye and look at the green balls for 10 seconds.

3. Close your left eye and look at the green crosses for 12 seconds.

4. Look with both eyes open at the bright green line for 20 seconds.

5. Look with both eyes open at the purple lines for 20 seconds.

6. Close your right eye and look at the orange ball on the left for 10 seconds.

7. Close your left eye and look at the orange ball on the right for 10 seconds.

8. Close your eyes and breathe mindfully for 20 seconds.

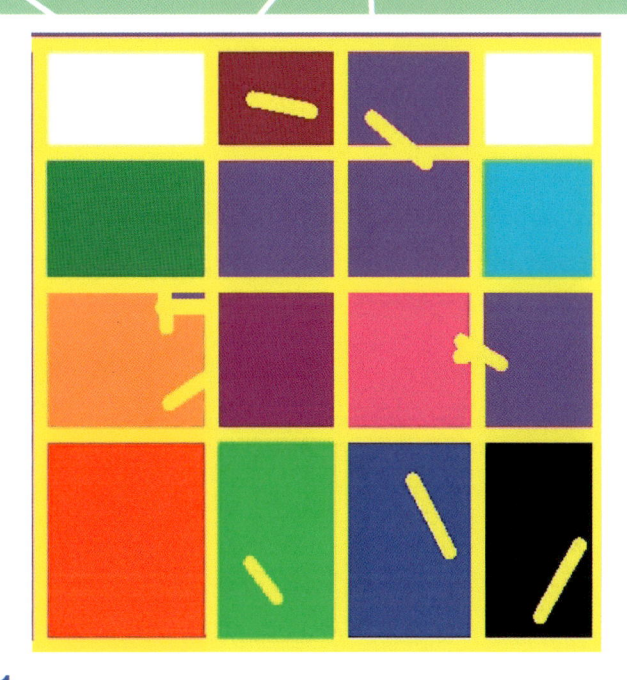

TEK 21

1. Sit comfortable and breathe mindfully for 21 seconds.

2. Close your right eye and look at the white block on the left for 22 seconds.

3. Close your left eye and look at the white block on the right for 23 seconds.

4. Look with both eyes open at the pink block for 24 seconds.

5. Look with both eyes open at the red block for 24 seconds.

6. Close your right eye and look at the orange block for 25 seconds.

7. Close your left eye and look at the orange block for 24 seconds.

8. Close your eyes and breathe mindfully for 21 seconds

TEK 22

1. Sit comfortable and breathe mindfully for 26 seconds.

2. Close your right eye and look at the brown object for 24 seconds.

3. Close your left eye and look at the brown object for 24 seconds.

4. Look with both eyes open at the purple object for 22 seconds.

5. Look with both eyes open at the three bright green balls for 20 seconds.

6. Close your right eye and look at the pink object for 18 seconds.

7. Close your left eye and look at the orange object for 18 seconds.

8. Close your eyes and breathe mindfully for 26 seconds.

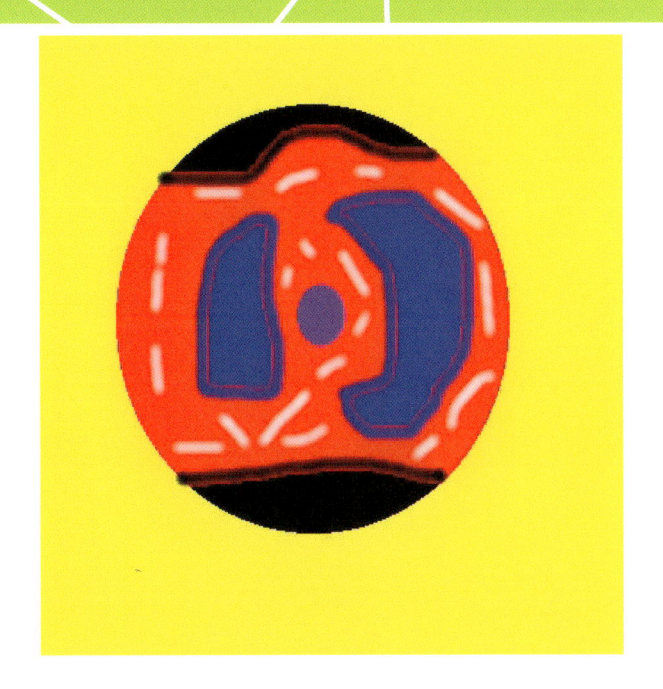

TEK 23

1. Sit comfortable and breathe mindfully for 27 seconds.

2. Close your right eye and look at the blue object on the left of the ball for 13 seconds.

3. Close your left eye and look at the blue object on the right of the ball for 13 seconds.

4. Look with both eyes open at the small white lines on the ball ball for 23 seconds.

5. Look with both eyes open at the ball for 21 seconds.

6. Close your right eye and look at the small purple ball in the middle for 13 seconds.

7. Close your left eye and look at the ball for 13 seconds.

8. Close your eyes and breathe mindfully for 28 seconds.

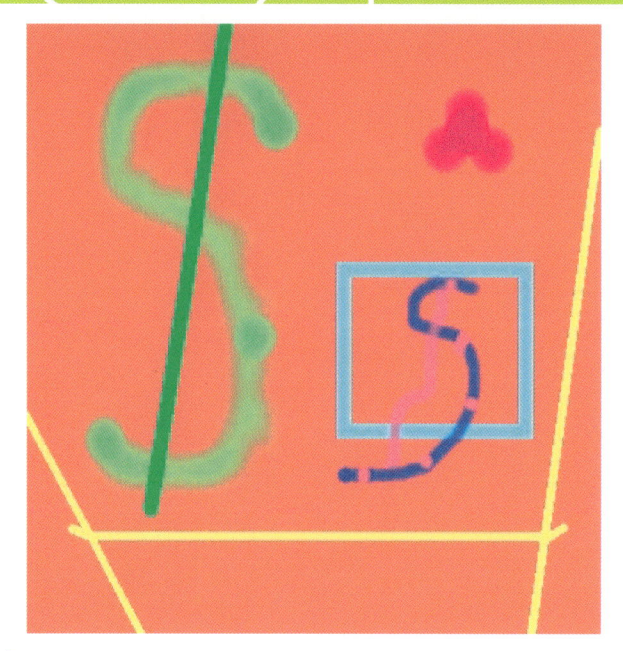

TEK 24

1. Sit comfortable and breathe mindfully for 29 seconds.

2. Close your right eye and look at the blue S for 23 seconds.

3. Close your left eye and look at the blue S for 13 seconds.

4. Look with both eyes open at the light blue square for 15 seconds.

5. Look with both eyes open at the yellow lines for 15 seconds.

6. Close your right eye and look at the big green S for 13 seconds.

7. Close your left eye and look at the big green S for 23 seconds.

8. Close your eyes and breathe mindfully for 29 seconds.

TEK 25

1. Sit comfortable and breathe mindfully for 30 seconds.

2. Close your right eye and look at the dark blue circle for 15 seconds.

3. Close your left eye and look at the red circle for 15 seconds.

4. Look with both eyes open at the blue arrow for 10 seconds.

5. Look with both eyes open at the green X for 10 seconds.

6. Close your right eye and look at the yellow egg for 15 seconds.

7. Close your left eye and look at the yellow egg for 15 seconds.

8. Close your eyes and breathe mindfully for 30 seconds.

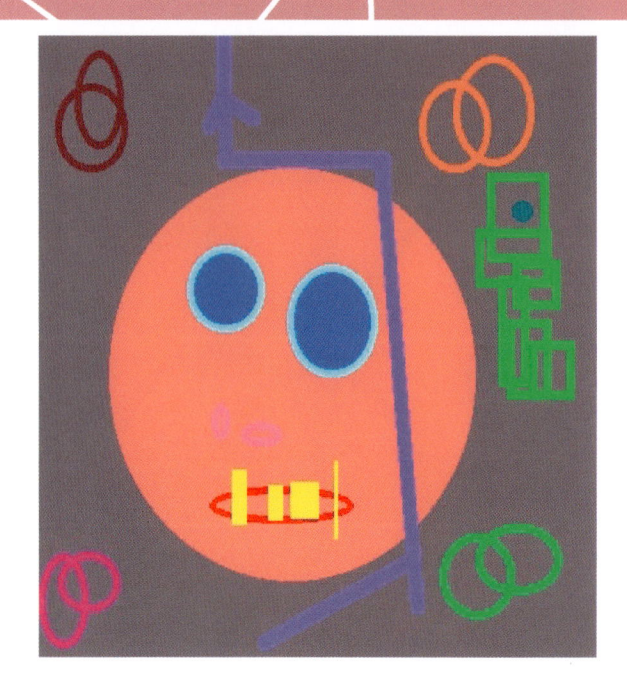

TEK 26

1. Sit comfortable and breathe mindfully for 2 seconds.

2. Close your right eye and look at the blue eye on the left for 12 seconds.

3. Close your left eye and look at the blue eye on the right for 13 seconds.

4. Look with both eyes open at the orange circles for 2 seconds.

5. Look with both eyes open at the pink circles for 3 seconds.

6. Close your right eye and look at the red mouth for 20 seconds.

7. Close your left eye and look at the yellow teeth for 20 seconds.

8. Close your eyes and breathe mindfully for 2 seconds.

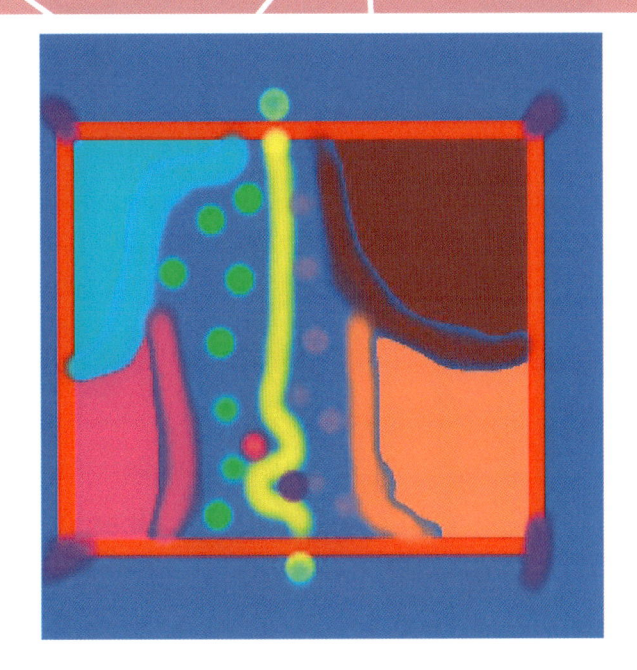

TEK 27

1. Sit comfortable and breathe mindfully for 30 seconds.

2. Close your right eye and look at the light blue object for 13 seconds.

3. Close your left eye and look at the orange object for 13 seconds.

4. Look with both eyes open at the purple ball for 20 seconds.

5. Look with both eyes open at the pink ball for 30 seconds.

6. Close your right eye and look at the yellow line for 13 seconds.

7. Close your left eye and look at the small green balls for 13 seconds.

8. Close your eyes and breathe mindfully for 30 seconds.

TEK 28

1. Sit comfortable and breathe mindfully for 4 seconds.

2. Close your right eye and look at the big blue object for 8 seconds.

3. Close your left eye and look at the big blue object for 8 seconds.

4. Look with both eyes open at the purple ball for 12 seconds.

5. Look with both eyes open at the green ball for 6 seconds.

6. Close your right eye and look at the white ball for 16 seconds.

7. Close your left eye and look at the yellow ball for 16 seconds.

8. Close your eyes and breathe mindfully for 4 seconds.

TEK 29

1. Sit comfortable and breathe mindfully for 20 seconds.

2. Close your right eye and look at the blue line for 16 seconds.

3. Close your left eye and look at the big white line for 16 seconds.

4. Look with both eyes open at the green circle for 24 seconds.

5. Look with both eyes open at the yellow object for 24 seconds.

6. Close your right eye and look at the pink object for 16 seconds.

7. Close your left eye and look at the red object for 16 seconds.

8. Close your eyes and breathe mindfully for 20 seconds.

TEK 30

1. Sit comfortable and breathe mindfully for 16 seconds.

2. Close your right eye and look at the blue ball for 16 seconds.

3. Close your left eye and look at the two pink balls on the right for 16 seconds.

4. Look with both eyes open at the pink ball in the middle for 16 seconds.

5. Look with both eyes open at the green ball for 16 seconds.

6. Close your right eye and look at the small red lines for 16 seconds.

7. Close your left eye and look at the small yellow lines for 16 seconds.

8. Close your eyes and breathe mindfully for 16 seconds.

TEK 31

1. Sit comfortable and breathe mindfully for 28 seconds.

2. Close your right eye and look at the light blue circle for 22 seconds.

3. Close your left eye and look at the blue circle for 22 seconds.

4. Look with both eyes open at the green block for 20 seconds.

5. Look with both eyes open at the blue block for 24 seconds.

6. Close your right eye and look at the yellow egg for 22 seconds.

7. Close your left eye and look at the pink ball for 22 seconds.

8. Close your eyes and breathe mindfully for 28 seconds.

TEK 32

1. Sit comfortable and breathe mindfully for 3 seconds.

2. Close your right eye and look at the blue object for 13 seconds.

3. Close your left eye and look at the big orange bug for 13 seconds.

4. Look with both eyes open at the purple object for 20 seconds.

5. Look with both eyes open at the green object for 3 seconds.

6. Close your right eye and look at the orange bug for 13 seconds.

7. Close your left eye and look at the pink object for 13 seconds.

8. Close your eyes and breathe mindfully for 3 seconds.

TEK 33

1. Sit comfortable and breathe mindfully for 6 seconds.

2. Close your right eye and look at the blue square for 9 seconds.

3. Close your left eye and look at the big face for 9 seconds.

4. Look with both eyes open at the black arrow for 12 seconds.

5. Look with both eyes open at the white arrow for 12 seconds.

6. Close your right eye and look at the purple ball for 15 seconds.

7. Close your left eye and look at the yellow arrow for 15 seconds.

8. Close your eyes and breathe mindfully for 6 seconds.

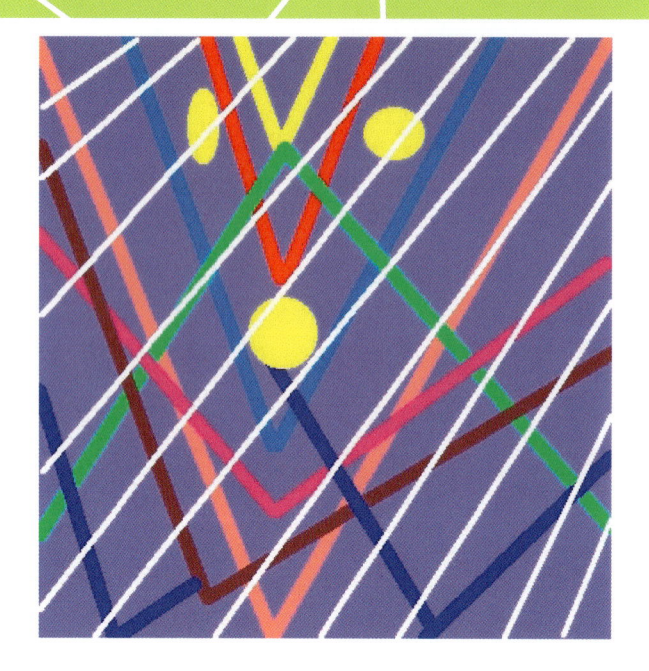

TEK 34

1. Sit comfortable and breathe mindfully for 13 seconds.

2. Close your right eye and look at the orange line for 13 seconds.

3. Close your left eye and look at the brown line for 13 seconds.

4. Look with both eyes open at the red line for 13 seconds.

5. Look with both eyes open at the pink line for 13 seconds.

6. Close your right eye and look at the green line for 13 seconds.

7. Close your left eye and look at the three yellow balls for 13 seconds.

8. Close your eyes and breathe mindfully for 13 seconds.

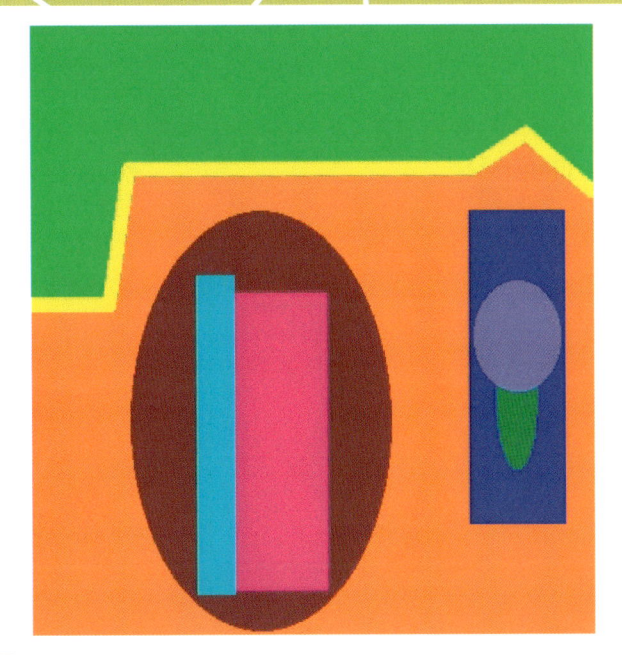

TEK 35

1. Sit comfortable and breathe mindfully for 18 seconds.

2. Close your right eye and look at the light blue object for 21 seconds.

3. Close your left eye and look at the pink object for 21 seconds.

4. Look with both eyes open at the purple ball for 20 seconds.

5. Look with both eyes open at the brown ball for 15 seconds.

6. Close your right eye and look at the yellow line for 24 seconds.

7. Close your left eye and look at the yellow line for 24 seconds.

8. Close your eyes and breathe mindfully for 26 seconds.

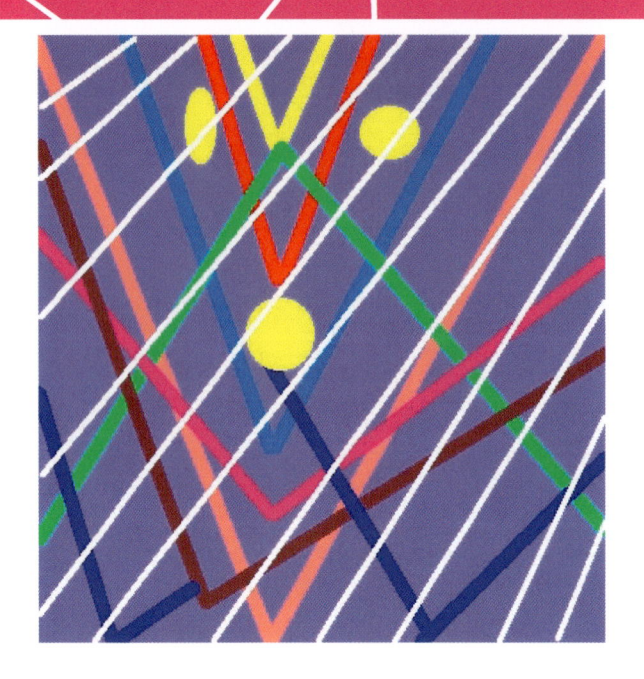

TEK 36

1. Sit comfortable and breathe mindfully for 27 seconds.

2. Close your right eye and look at the brown line for 30 seconds.

3. Close your left eye and look at the green line for 30 seconds.

4. Look with both eyes open at the big yellow ball in the middle for 3 seconds.

5. Look with both eyes open at the three yellow balls for 3 seconds.

6. Close your right eye and look at the bright pink line for 30 seconds.

7. Close your left eye and look at the green line for 30 seconds.

8. Close your eyes and breathe mindfully for 27 seconds.

TEK 37

1. Sit comfortable and breathe mindfully for 5 seconds.

2. Close your right eye and look at the green arrow for 5 seconds.

3. Close your left eye and look at the bright pink line for 5 seconds.

4. Look with both eyes open at the pink ball for 5 seconds.

5. Look with both eyes open at the yellow line for 5 seconds.

6. Close your right eye and look at the red line for 5 seconds.

7. Close your left eye and look at the orange face for 5 seconds.

8. Close your eyes and breathe mindfully for 5 seconds.

TEK 38

1. Sit comfortable and breathe mindfully for 10 seconds.

2. Close your right eye and look at the big blue ball on the top of the roof for 15 seconds.

3. Close your left eye and look at pink window for 15 seconds.

4. Look with both eyes open at the four small black balls for 10 seconds.

5. Look with both eyes open at the house for 10 seconds.

6. Close your right eye and look at the red window for 20 seconds.

7. Close your left eye and look at the orange door for 20 seconds.

8. Close your eyes and breathe mindfully for 10 seconds.

TEK 39

1. Sit comfortable and breathe mindfully for 25 seconds.

2. Close your right eye and look at the pink object for 30 seconds.

3. Close your left eye and look at the pink object for 30 seconds.

4. Look with both eyes open at the blue background for 25 seconds.

5. Look with both eyes open at the red object for 25 seconds.

6. Close your right eye and look at the yellow object for 30 seconds.

7. Close your left eye and look at the yellow object for 30 seconds.

8. Close your eyes and breathe mindfully for 25 seconds.

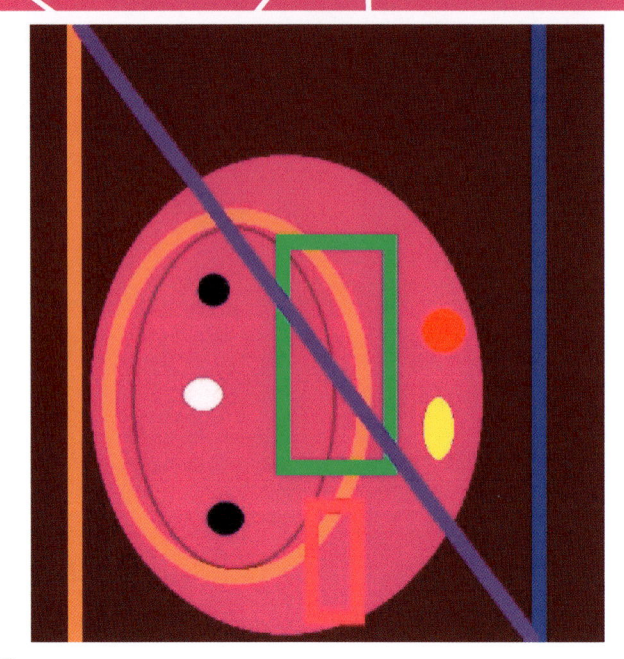

TEK 40

1. Sit comfortable and breathe mindfully for 6 seconds.

2. Close your right eye and look at the blue line for 6 seconds.

3. Close your left eye and look at the purple line for 6 seconds.

4. Look with both eyes open at the green rectangle for 12 seconds.

5. Look with both eyes open at the orange circle for 12 seconds.

6. Close your right eye and look at the orange line for 6 seconds.

7. Close your left eye and look at the happy, smiling face for 6 seconds.

8. Close your eyes and breathe mindfully for 6 seconds.

Printed in Germany
by Amazon Distribution
GmbH, Leipzig